ALTO SAX

50 ESSENTIAL BEBOP HEADS

This publication is not for sale in
the E.C. and/or Australia
or New Zealand.

ISBN 0-7935-5993-6

**HAL•LEONARD®
CORPORATION**

7777 W. BLUEMOUND RD. P.O. BOX 13819 MILWAUKEE, WI 53213

Copyright © 1996 by HAL LEONARD CORPORATION
International Copyright Secured   All Rights Reserved

For all works contained herein:
Unauthorized copying, arranging, adapting, recording or public performance is an infringement of copyright.
Infringers are liable under the law.

FOREWORD

The style of music called bebop (or known variously as rebop, or just plain bop) was first heard in casual jam sessions performed in the early '40s by such musicians as Charlie (Bird) Parker, Dizzy Gillespie, Charlie Christian, Thelonious Monk, Bud Powell and Kenny Clarke. The music is made up of intricate melodies (often harmonically similar, or identical to, many standard songs of earlier years), and an entirely different approach in the rhythm section. In earlier styles of jazz, the drums would play a consistent, steady beat. In bop, the bass keeps the steady pulse, while the piano and drums play accents and punctuations (often called bombs). Harmonically, there is much use of altered notes in chords, such as augmented 9ths and 11ths, or flatted 5ths. Very often, heads are played in unison rather than in harmony.

Even though bop is primarily known as a small group jazz style, several big bands adapted the new style to their music. Such bands as Billy Eckstine's, Dizzy Gillespie's, Woody Herman's and even Charlie Barnet's and Les Brown's featured the elements of bop extensively in the late '40s.

The music continued to evolve in the '50s and '60s, and split off in many directions such as cool and hard bop.

50 ESSENTIAL BEBOP HEADS
ARRANGED FOR ALTO SAX

4 Afternoon in Paris		
5 Ah-Leu-Cha		
4 Another Hairdo		
6 Anthropology		
7 Au Privave	15 Dewey Square	30 A Night in Tunisia
7 Back Home Blues	18 Dizzy Atmosphere	28 Now's the Time
8 Barbados	17 Donna Lee	29 Ornithology
8 Bebop	20 Epistrophy	31 Passport
9 Billie's Bounce	19 Five Brothers	32 Quicksilver
10 Bird Feathers	21 Four Brothers	34 Red Cross
10 Bloomdido	20 Groovin' High	33 S.O.S.
11 Blue 'n Boogie	22 Half Nelson	34 Salt Peanuts
12 Blues for Alice	24 Kim	35 Scrapple from the Apple
12 Boplicity (Bebop Lives)	25 Ko Ko	36 Some Other Blues
13 Byrd Like	26 Lennie's Pennies	36 Steeplechase
14 Chasing the Bird	23 Mayreh	37 Things to Come
14 Cheryl	22 Mohawk	38 Thriving from a Riff
18 Chi Chi	27 Moose the Mooche	40 26-2
16 Confirmation	28 Mr. P.C.	38 Well You Needn't (It's Over Now)
		39 Woody 'n You

Another Hairdo

By Charlie Parker

Alto Sax

Uptempo Blues

Copyright © 1948 (Renewed 1976) Atlantic Music Corp.
International Copyright Secured   All Rights Reserved

Afternoon in Paris

By John Lewis

Alto Sax

Moderate Swing

Copyright © 1955 (Renewed 1983) by MJQ Music, Inc.
International Copyright Secured   All Rights Reserved

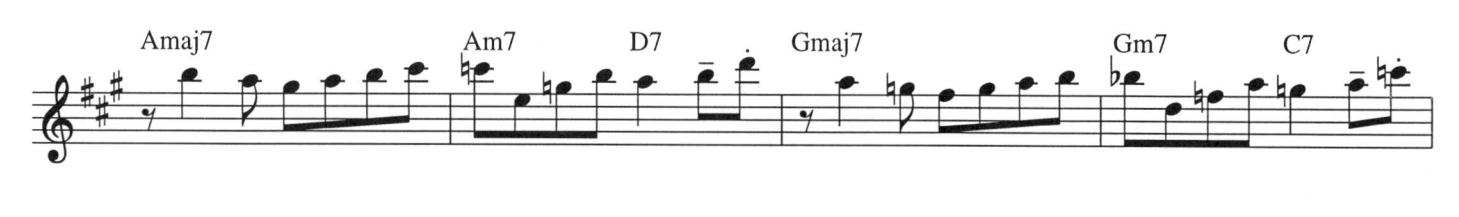

Ah-Leu-Cha

By Charlie Parker

Alto Sax

Anthropology

By Charlie Parker and Dizzy Gillespie

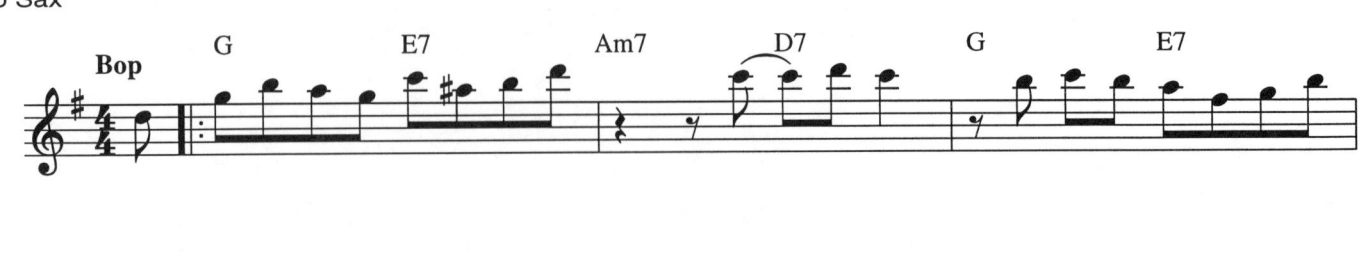

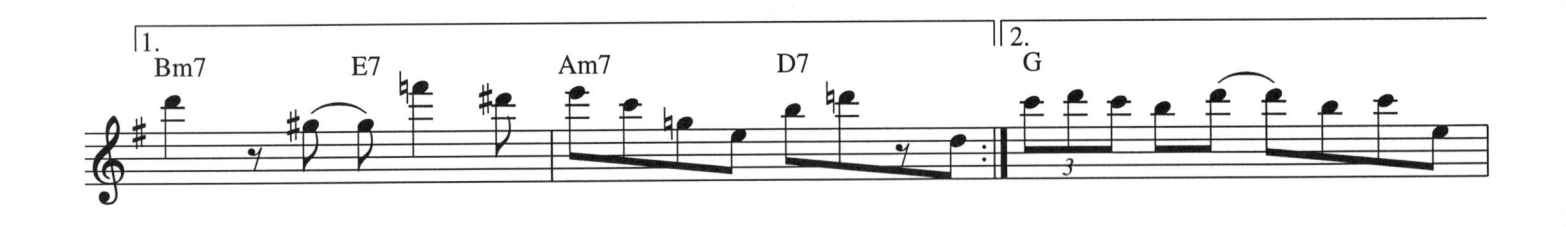

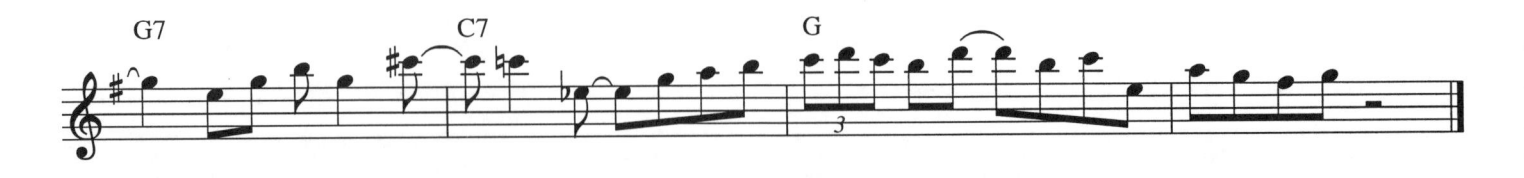

Au Privave

By Charlie Parker

Barbados

By Charlie Parker

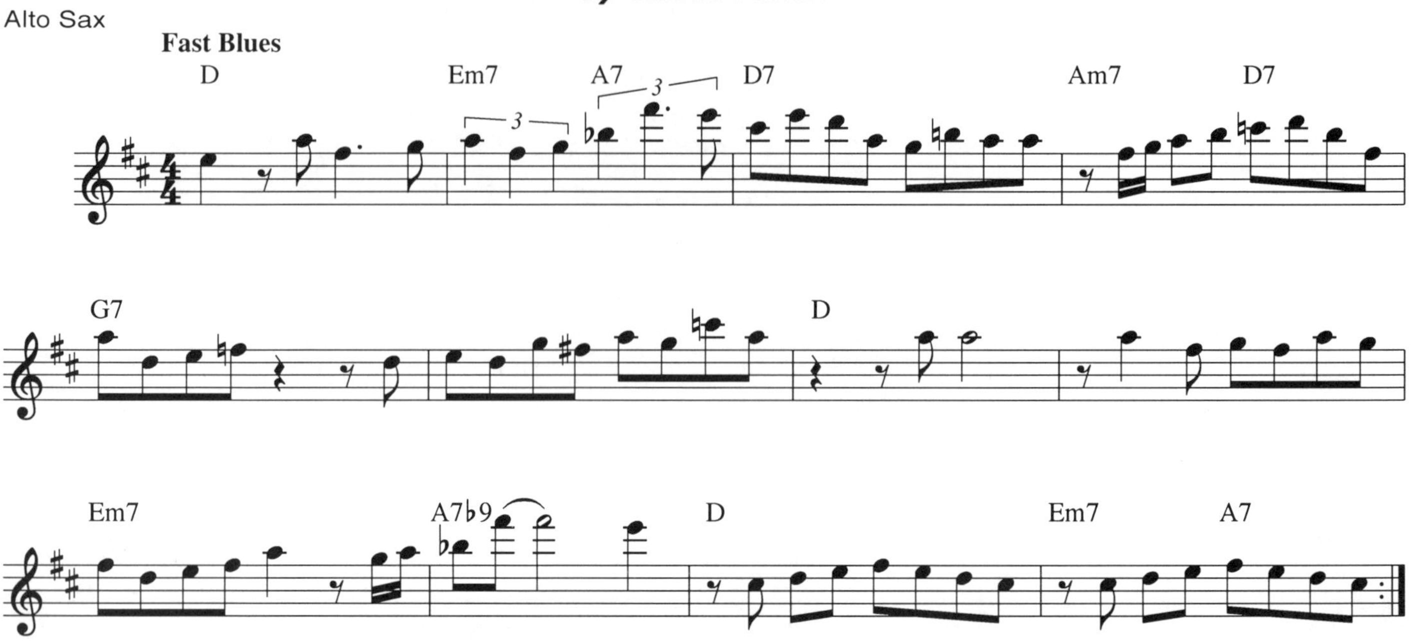

Bebop

By John "Dizzy" Gillespie

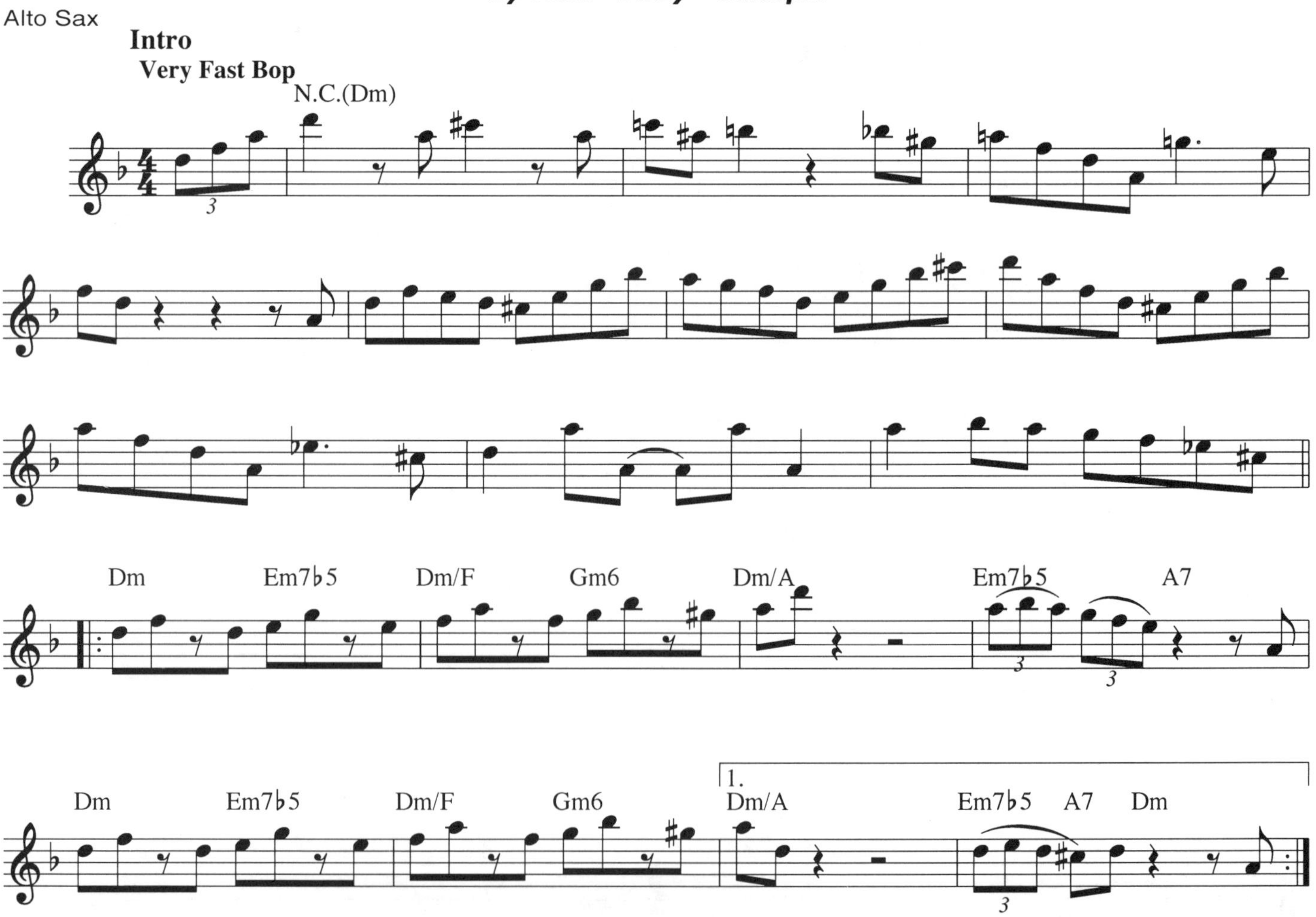

Billie's Bounce
By Charlie Parker

Bird Feathers

By Charlie Parker

Alto Sax

Fast Bop

Bloomdido

By Charlie Parker

Alto Sax

Very Fast Blues

Blue 'n Boogie

Music by John "Dizzy" Gillespie and Frank Paparelli

Alto Sax

Blues for Alice

By Charlie Parker

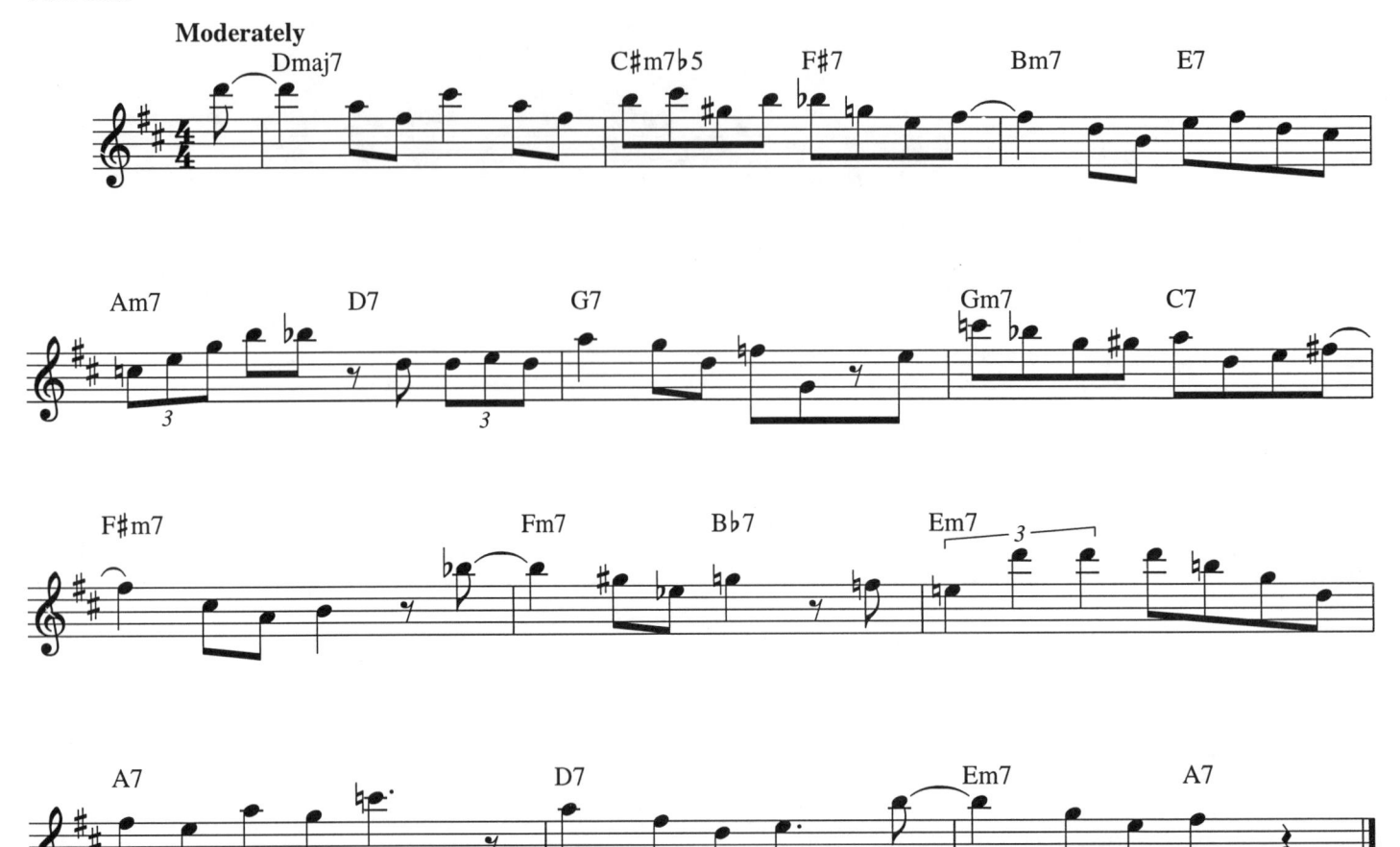

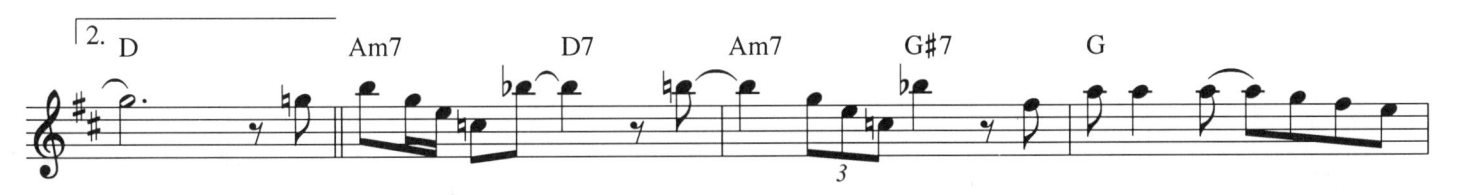

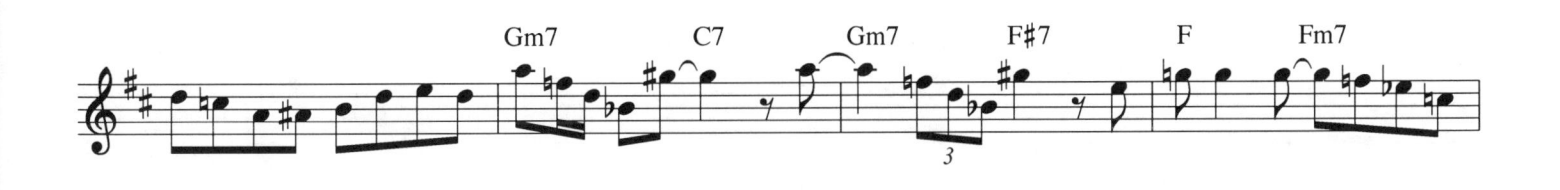

Byrd Like
By Freddie Hubbard

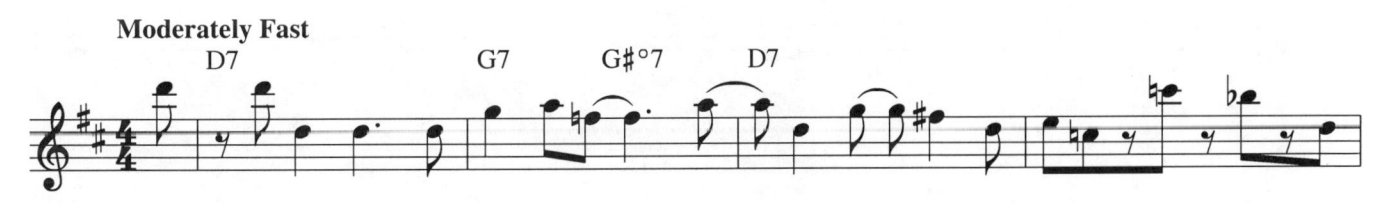

Cheryl

By Charlie Parker

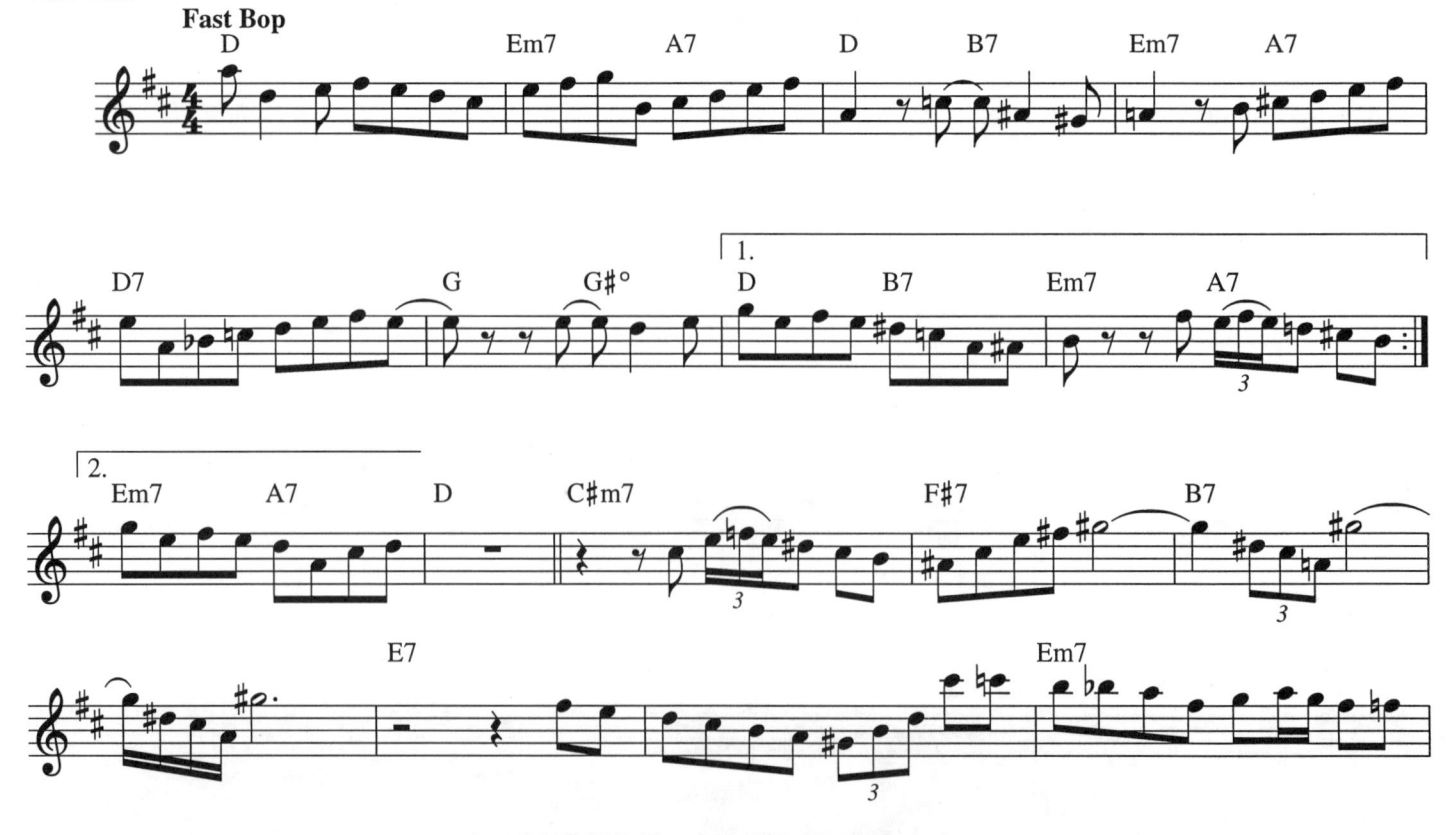

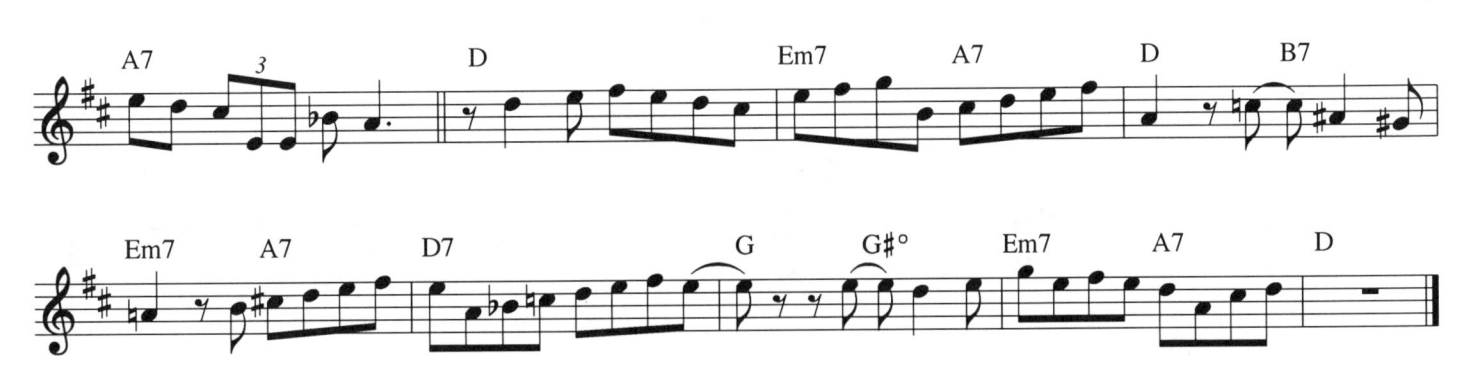

Dewey Square
By Charlie Parker

Confirmation

By Charlie Parker

Alto Sax

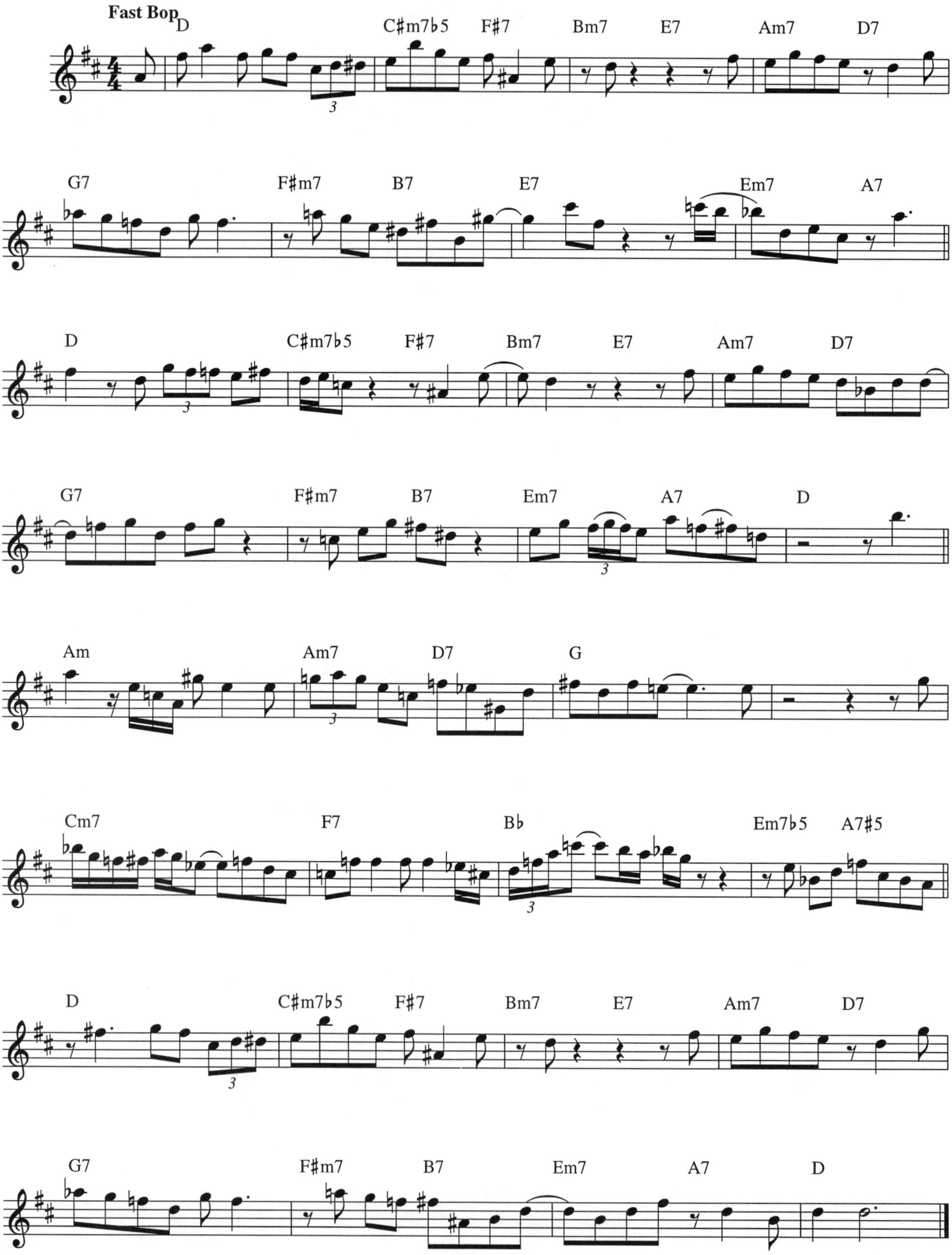

Donna Lee

By Charlie Parker

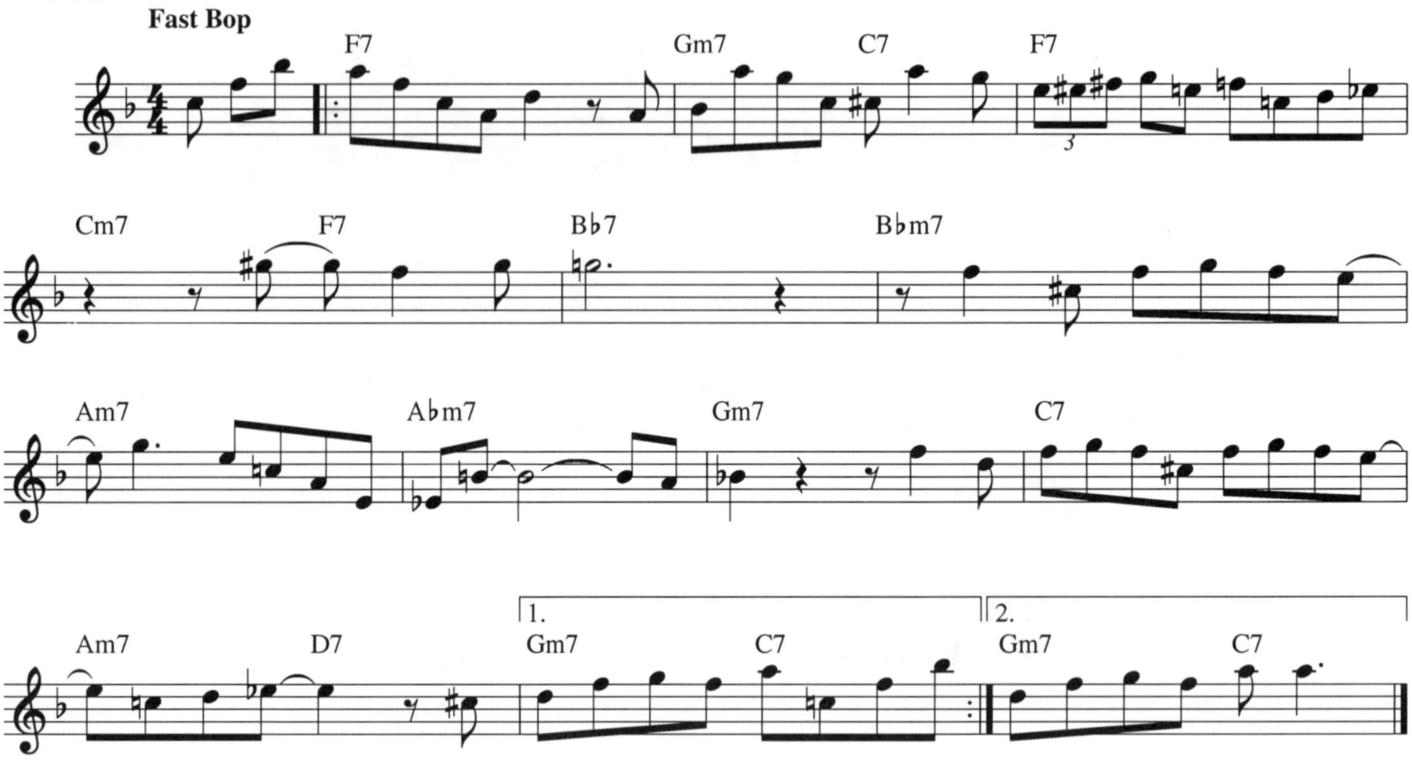

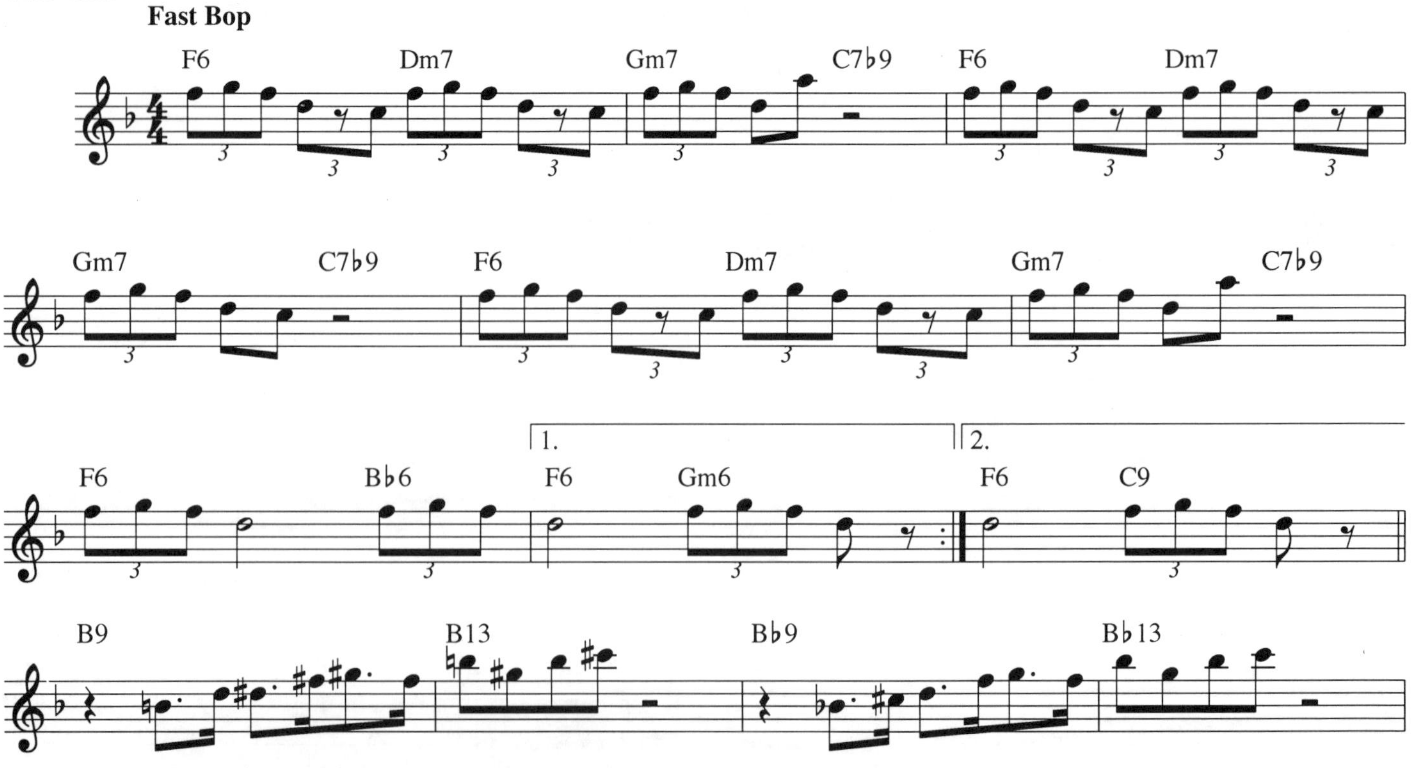

Five Brothers
By Gerry Mulligan

Alto Sax

© 1949 (Renewed 1977) BEECHWOOD MUSIC CORP.
All Rights Reserved   International Copyright Secured   Used by Permission

Groovin' High

By Dizzy Gillespie

Alto Sax

Epistrophy

By Thelonious Monk and Kenny Clark

Alto Sax

Four Brothers

By Jimmy Giuffre

Alto Sax

Mohawk

By Charlie Parker

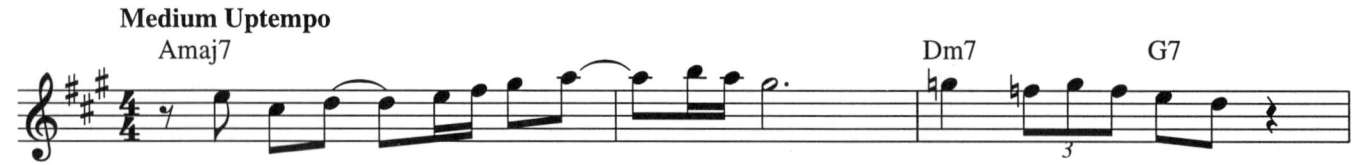

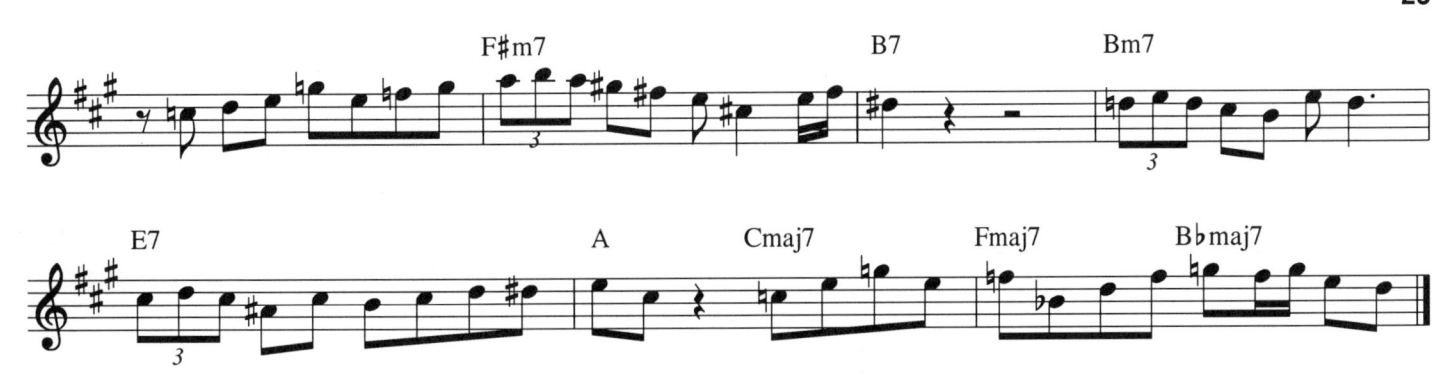

Mayreh
By Horace Silver

Kim

By Charlie Parker

Alto Sax

Very Fast Bop

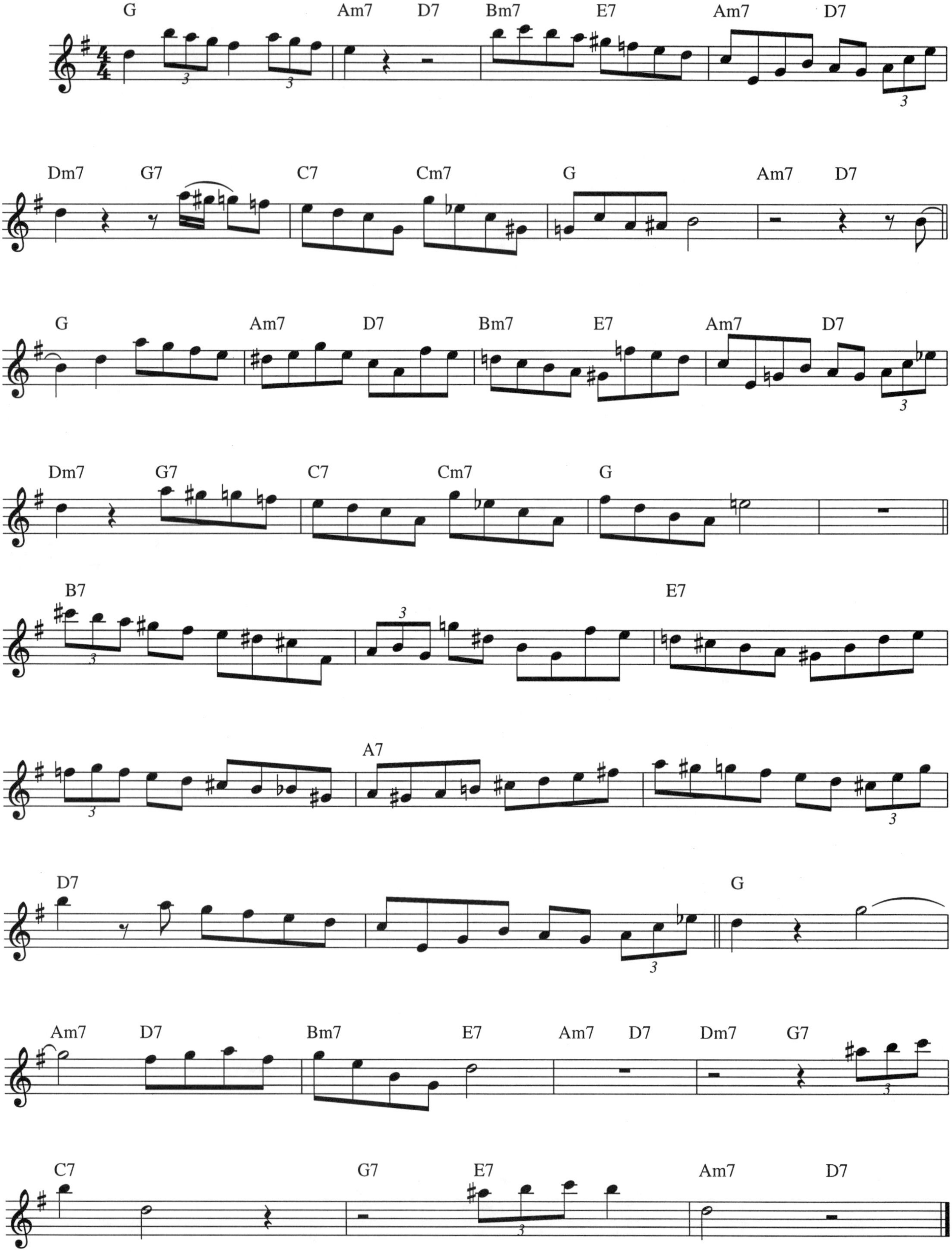

Ko Ko

By Charlie Parker

Lennie's Pennies

By Lennie Tristano

Alto Sax

Moose the Mooche

By Charlie Parker

Mr. P.C.

By John Coltrane

Ornithology

By Charlie Parker and Benny Harris

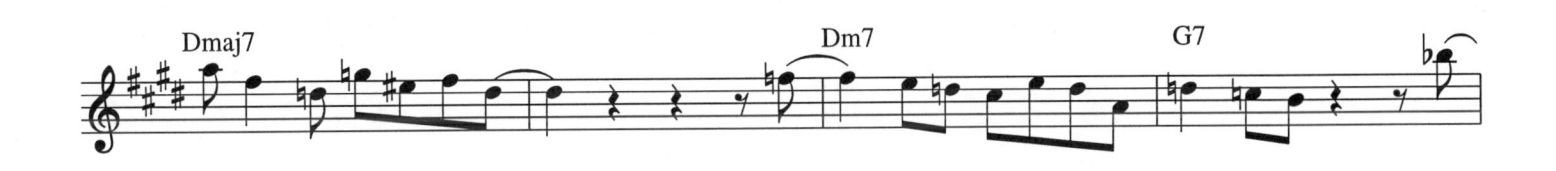

Alto Sax

A Night in Tunisia

Music by John "Dizzy" Gillespie and Frank Paparelli

Alto Sax

Passport

By Charlie Parker

Quicksilver

By Horace Silver

Alto Sax

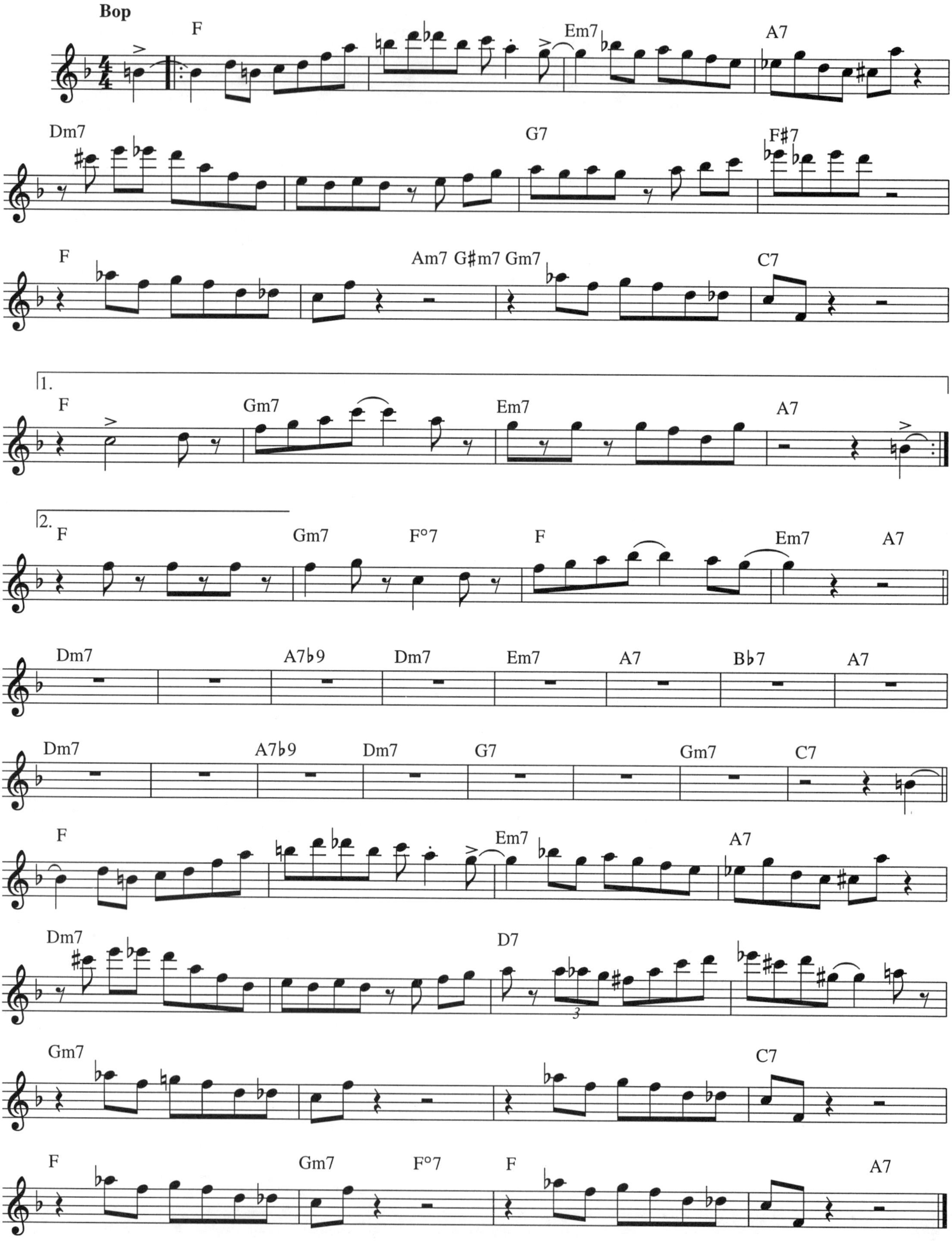

S.O.S.

By John L. "Wes" Montgomery

Alto Sax

Red Cross

By Charlie Parker

Alto Sax

Salt Peanuts

Music by John "Dizzy" Gillespie and Kenny Clarke

Alto Sax

Scrapple from the Apple
By Charlie Parker

Some Other Blues

By John Coltrane

Alto Sax

Steeplechase

By Charlie Parker

Alto Sax

Things to Come

By Dizzy Gillespie and Gil Fuller

Alto Sax

Well You Needn't (It's Over Now)

Music by Thelonius Monk

Alto Sax

Thriving from a Riff

By Charlie Parker

Alto Sax

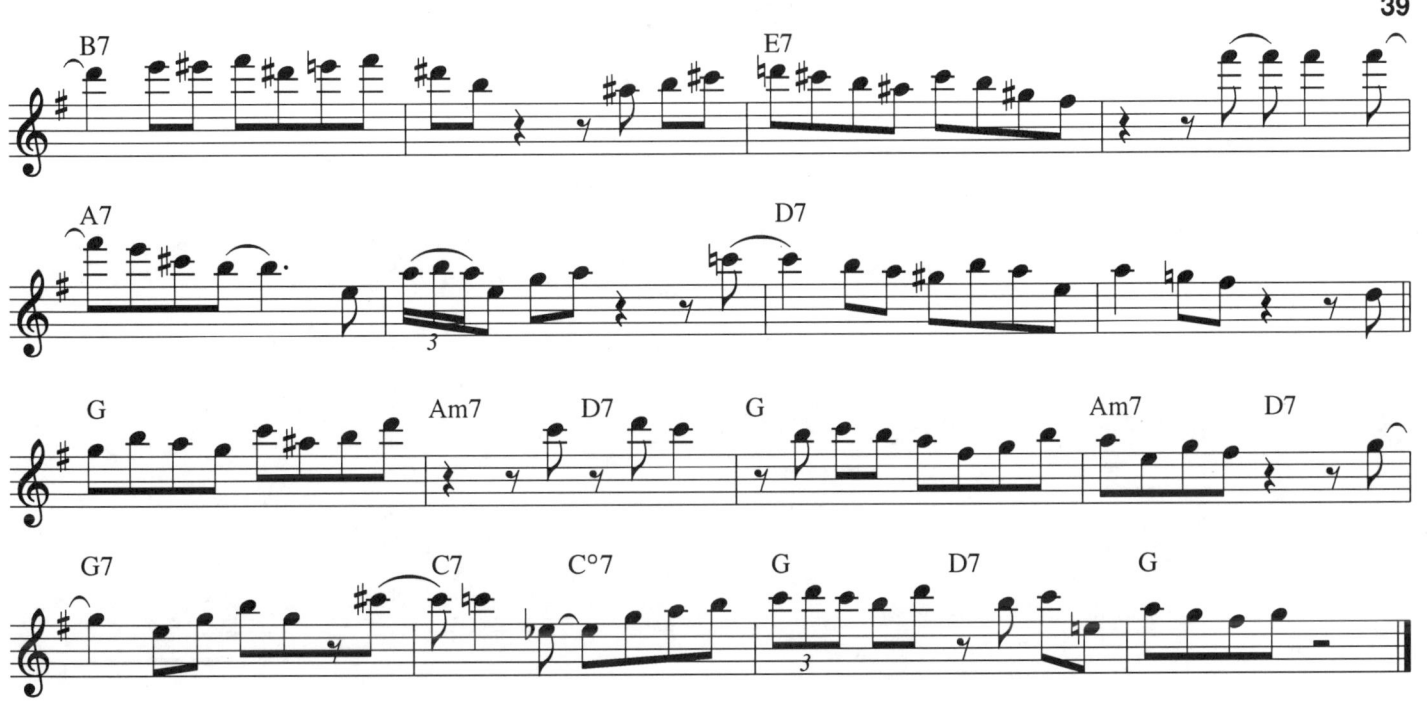

Woody 'n You
By Dizzy Gillespie

26-2

By John Coltrane

Alto Sax

Fast Bop

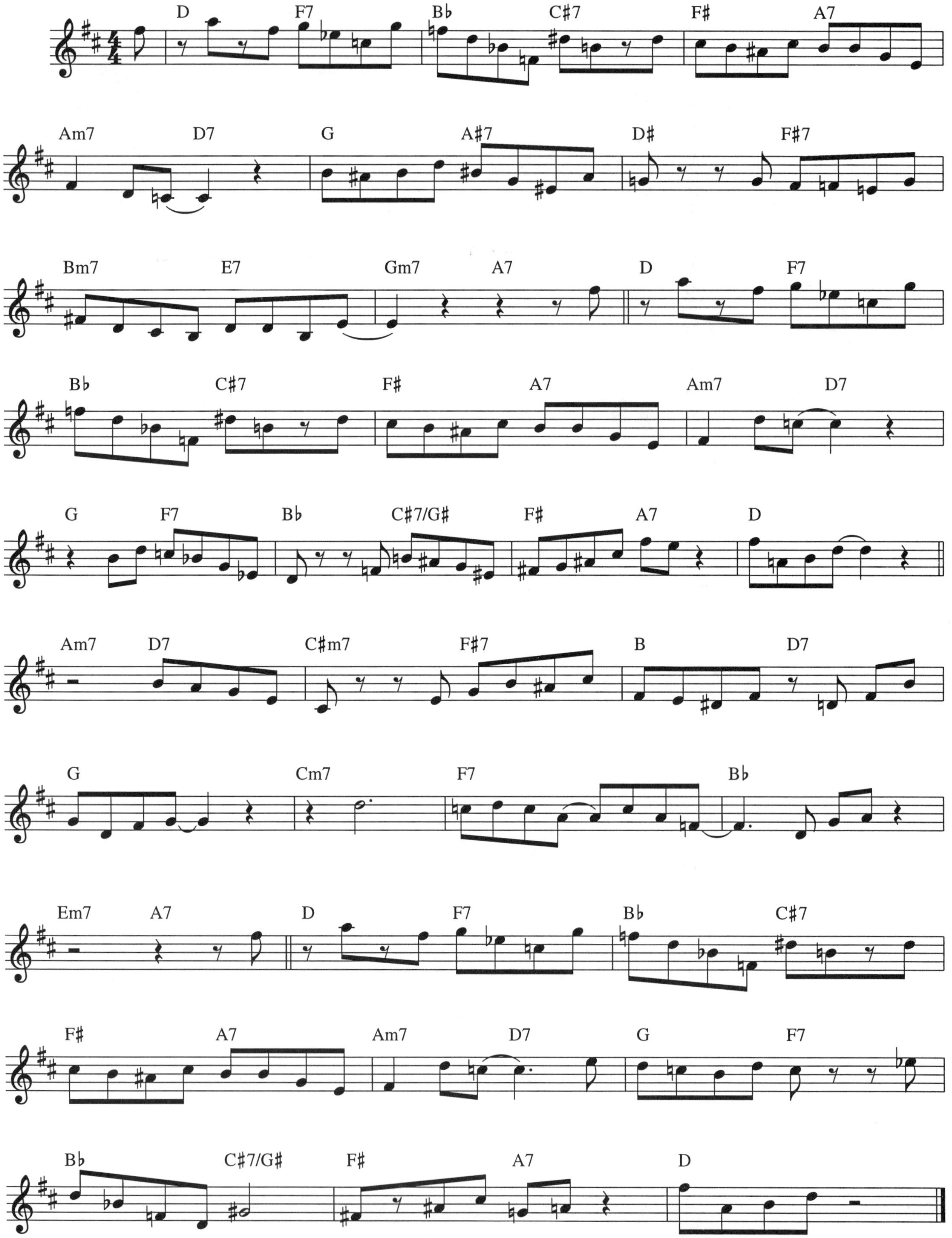